Encyclopedia of
Places

CELEBRATION PRESS

Pearson Learning Group

Contents

Beach   4

Desert   6

Forest   8

Mountains   10

Pond   12

Tundra   14

Index   16

The world has many places.
Find out about some of them in this book.

Beach

All beaches have shores.

Things Found at Some Beaches

seaweed

shell

sand

sea gull

pebbles

starfish

Desert

All deserts are dry.

Things Found in Some Deserts

camel

sand dune

lizard

scorpion

cactus

oasis

Forest

All forests have trees.

Things Found in Some Forests

pine cone

beetle

ferns

woodpecker

mushrooms

squirrel

Mountains

All mountains are tall.

Things Found on Some Mountains

snow

goat

eagle

plant

bear

mountain peak

Pond

All ponds have water.

Things Found in Some Ponds

frog

snail

fish

reeds

waterlily

dragonfly

Tundra

All tundra are cold.

Things Found on Some Tundra

snowshoe hare

snow goose

alpine fleabane flowers

musk ox

reindeer moss

reindeer

Index

beach...4–5

desert...6–7

forest...8–9

mountains.......................................10–11

pond..12–13

tundra...14–15